Keeping the Dream Alive

Keeping the Dream Alive

Reflections on the Art of Harriet Lorence Nesbitt

EDITED BY
JEANNE C. DEFAZIO

FOREWORD BY
Julia C. Davis, Olga Soler, Dr. Martha Reyes

AFTERWORD BY
William David Spencer

RESOURCE *Publications* • Eugene, Oregon

KEEPING THE DREAM ALIVE
Reflections on the Art of Harriet Lorence Nesbitt

Resource Publications
An Imprint of Wipf and Stock Publishers
199 W. 8th Ave., Suite 3
Eugene, OR 97401

www.wipfandstock.com

PAPERBACK ISBN: 978-1-5326-8428-9
HARDCOVER ISBN: 978-1-5326-8429-6
EBOOK ISBN: 978-1-5326-8430-2

Manufactured in the U.S.A. MAY 21, 2019

This book is dedicated to Harriet Lorence Nesbitt,
award-winning New York City artist,
Politics and Such columnist and
founder of Mothers for More Halfway Houses.

A true friend who made me want to be a better person.

By the Same Authors

Julia C. Davis

Empowering English Language Learners: Successful Strategies of Christian Educators (contributing author)

Jeanne C. DeFazio

Creative Ways to Build Christian Community (edited with John P. Lathrop)
How to Have an Attitude of Gratitude on the Night Shift (with Teresa Flowers)
Redeeming the Screens: Living Stories of Media "Ministers" Bringing the Message of Jesus Christ to the Entertainment Industry (edited with William David Spencer)
Berkeley Street Theatre: How Improvisation and Street Theater Emerged as Christian Outreach to the Culture of the Time (editor)
Empowering English Language Learners: Successful Strategies of Christian Educators (edited with William David Spencer)

Martha Reyes

Jesús y la Mujer Herida (*Jesus and the Wounded Woman*)
Jesucristo, Tu Psicólogo Personal (*Jesus Is Your Own Personal Psychologist*)
Por Que No Soy Feliz (*Why Am I Not Happy?*)

Olga Soler

Just Don't Marry One: Interracial Dating, Marriage, and Parenting (contributing author)
Tough Inspirations from the Weeping Prophet
Apocalypse of Youth (Artist Harriet Nesbitt as told to Olga Soler)
Creative Ways to Build Christian Community (contributing author)

*Epistle to the Magadalenes (*author and illustrator)
Redeeming the Screens: Living Stories of Media "Ministers" Bringing the Message of Jesus Christ to the Entertainment Industry (contributing author)
Berkeley Street Theatre: How Improvisation and Street Theater Emerged as Christian Outreach to the Culture of the Time (contributing author)
The First Book: Nature; The Second Book: Time Travel, Adventure, Romance, Faith; The Third Book: Revelation: Revelations Series
Empowering English Language Learners: Successful Strategies of Christian Educators (contributing author)

William David Spencer

Name in the Papers: Eleven Snapshots and a Video (novel)
Mysterium and Mystery: The Minister as Detective in the Clerical Crime Novel
Dread Jesus
Redeeming the Screens: Living Stories of Media "Ministers" Bringing the Message of Jesus Christ to the Entertainment Industry (edited with Jeanne C. DeFazio)
God through the Looking Glass: Glimpses from the Arts
(edited with Aída Besançon Spencer)
Marriage at the Crossroads: Couples in Conversation about Discipleship, Gender Roles, Decision Making and Intimacy
(with Aída Besançon Spencer, Steven R. Tracy, and Celestia G. Tracy)
Joy through the Night: Biblical Resources on Suffering (with Aída Besançon Spencer)
The Prayer Life of Jesus: Shout of Agony, Revelation of Love
(with Aída Besançon Spencer)
Global Voices on Biblical Equality: Women and Men Serving Together in the Church (ed. with Aída Besançon Spencer and Mimi Haddad)
Reaching for the New Jerusalem: A Biblical and Theological Framework for the City (edited with Seong Hyun Park and Aída Besançon Spencer)
The Global God: Multicultural Evangelical Views of God
(edited with Aída Besançon Spencer)
The Goddess Revival: A Christian Response
(with Aída Besançon Spencer, Donna G.F. Hailson, and Catherine Clark Kroeger)
Chanting Down Babylon: The Rastafari Reader
(ed. with Nathaniel Samuel Murrell and Adrian Anthony McFarlane)

2 Corinthians: A Commentary (with Aída Besançon Spencer)
Empowering English Language Learners: Successful Strategies of Christian Educators (edited with Jeanne DeFazio)
Cave of Little Faces: A Novel (with Aída Besançon Spencer)

Contents

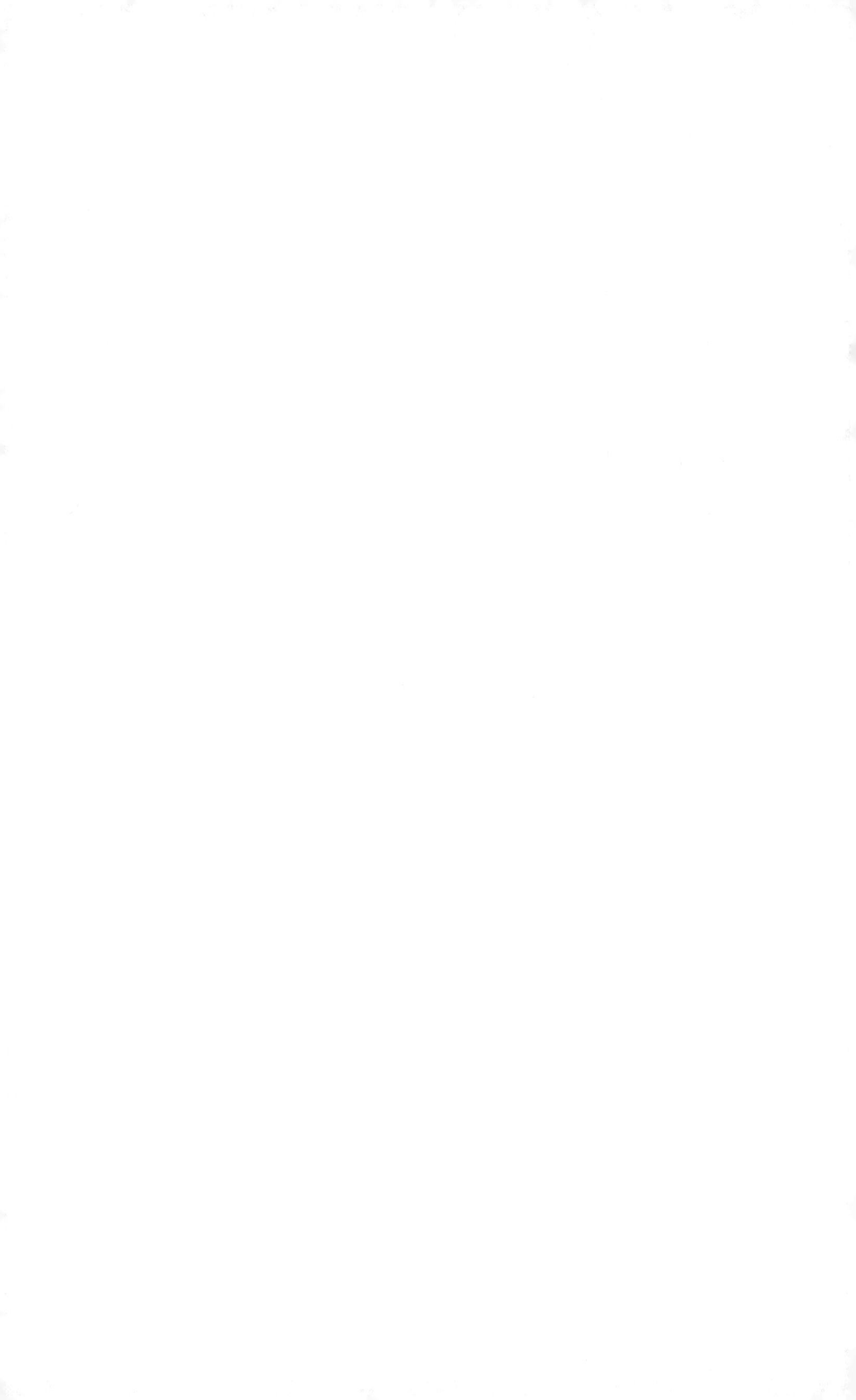

Foreword

Julia C. Davis

This book is part of the legacy of Harriet Nesbitt's son Larry Nesbitt, a young scholar with extraordinary promise. Larry, like many of my students, suffered from a psychological disorder. I firmly believe that each Special Education, ELL, and mainstream student has unique God-given ability which can be nurtured toward success in the correct learning environment. As a Special Education teacher with over thirty years of experience teaching in New York, Maryland, and Washington, DC inner city public schools, I am participating in this dialogue to identify art appreciation as a teaching strategy suited to the learning needs of "at risk" and Special Education students.[1]

It has been my experiences that Special Education students learn effectively through the arts. Participation in creative arts reduces stress, which in turn enhances the ability to learn. David Graham, in his article "Inclusion Strategies for Mainstreamed Classrooms," explains: "The environment is the common cause of a broad continuum of mental health problems in students."[2]Art therapy can reduce the stress that contributes to mental health problems.

Art appreciation is a successful strategy for teaching Special Education students. In the summer of 2018, as the founder of Education Matters Associates, I developed a program for students and their families to tour The Harvard Semitic Museum's Israel and Egyptian exhibits. I prepared and distributed resource materials to meet the students' individual needs. This program engaged English Language Learners, the Special Education

1. Julia C. Davis, "Strategies That Are Scripturally Based for the Public-School Classroom," in DeFazio and Spender, eds., *Empowering English Language Learners*, 35.

2. Farnsworth, "Interventions."

student, and the mainstream student.[3] Exploring The Harvard Semitic Museum advanced student comprehension of art. Participation in group discussions with Adam Middleton improved students' ability to follow a multilevel discussion. Question-and-answer time with Adam Middleton improved each student's ability to use "I" statements to describe art and artifacts, as well as to describe the color, style, and function of art and artifacts. Students' ability to use appropriate third-person pronouns to describe artwork increased. Group discussion enhanced students' understanding of art. Touring the Israel and Egyptian Exhibit of The Harvard Semitic Museum encouraged the students to differentiate between art textures (wet, dry, sticky) and medium. Students' cognitive as well as fine motor skills improved. Giving Special Education students, English Language Learners, and mainstream students the opportunity to explore art together is a very effective social inclusion strategy. In the study and appreciation of art there is more than one right answer. Students who are allowed to view art as a group have the opportunity to appreciate and enjoy each other and art—"that's social inclusion at its best."[4] I want to extend my gratitude for the support of Harvard professor Dr. Ali Asani, and Adam Middleton, The Harvard Semitic Museum coordinator, who allowed me to bring students to The Harvard Semitic Museum as part of EMA's cultural studies program.

Julia C. Davis
Telephone: 781-393-4517
Email: jdavis.ema@gmail.com

3. Wang, "Special Education."

4. Farnsworth, "Interventions."

Olga Soler

I HAD THE HONOR to publish Harriet's memoirs, *Apocalypse of Youth*. I want to encourage readers to get the book on Amazon and to read more about Harriet's inspiring life. I am participating in this dialogue to identify art as an antidote for loneliness and depression. Madeline R. Vann, MPH, in her article "Dealing with Depression and Loneliness," explains:

> Everyone feels lonely from time to time, but for some, loneliness comes far too often. Feeling lonely can plague many people, including the elderly, people who are isolated, and those with depression, with symptoms such as sadness, isolation, and withdrawal.[1]

In *Creative Ways to Build Christian Community*, I described an art event that promoted inclusion and was a lot of fun!

> We had a techno event at the arts place one night that was a great example of these points. It was the night before Easter Sunday, and we wanted to do a resurrection theme. Our theater had all black walls and an all-black ceiling, as many theaters do. We placed a slab on a desk and put it on the stage. We placed ultraviolet lights everywhere. The music started. As people came in, we asked them to take some chalk and draw their idea of angels on the walls. These were illuminated by the black light, giving them an otherworldly effect. We had other people working on a mural which depicted the opening of a cave with a view of the dawn in it. We lit the installation so that the light appeared to be entering in from outside the cave. An installation is a sculpture that takes up a whole area, sort of like an artistic biosphere. On the slab we had other people building a man. They stuffed clothes till we had the shape of a man and then wound bandages around him. The bandages were of a white shiny material that caught the light nicely. After we wound him like a mummy, we took the tail of all the bandages and draped them over the pipes on the ceiling. It gave them the appearance of floating in the air, as if they were coming off of the body by themselves. We then strewed red roses all over the installation, and along with the floating bandages we had chains that were also sort of floating off of the body. The people did not know what they were doing or why, but those of us who were believers had the opportunity to speak to them a little here and there as we worked.

1. Vann, "Dealing with Depression and Loneliness."

> We were instructed not to talk too much. The piece spoke for itself. We called it moments before dawn on the 1st day. The dead man was, of course, Christ, and the bandages and chains were falling off of him because death was leaving him as the resurrection began to take place. The roses were symbols of the love that made it all possible. When it was all over, everyone found themselves in the middle of the tomb with Christ about to rise from the dead. The anticipation was palpable. Was this all too weird for people to understand? We heard one not yet believing girl remark as she stared at the finished work, Oh poor, poor Jesus! The message was obviously hitting the mark with her and with others.[2]

This event was social inclusion at its best. I want to encourage readers to use art activities to inform, promote inclusion, prevent loneliness and depression, and for fun!

Olga Soler
Email: fleursavag@aol.com

2. DeFazio and Lathrop, eds., *Creative Ways*, 52, 53.

Dr. Martha Reyes

I met Harriet Lorence Nesbitt in the 1980s when I was a guest speaker at one of the Reverend Robert Rieth's Media Fellowship International luncheons in New York City.[1] I hold a doctorate in clinical psychology and I am the founder of Hosanna Foundation, which offers counseling, support groups, and courses on depression, married life, self-esteem, women and their families, victims of abuse, violence, and addictions.

As I shared in my chapter "Healing Through Faith and Compassion," in *Redeeming the Screens*:

> Make no mistake, I have not only been one of the healers, I have also been broken and in need of healing myself. But I have also discovered the virtue of undeserved brokenness and the power of the wounded healer. That is the greatest gift of love: not giving leftovers for care but breaking our own bread and our own life in smaller parts to share with those who have nothing (e.g., as Phil 1:13-14, Paul the Apostle notes that, because of his chains, others have been encouraged and blessed). I guess during different stages in my life, I have played the role of every character in the Good Samaritan parable (except the bandits!) because, before I felt God's calling in my life, I was also disconnected and dissociated from other people's needs. Just like the indifferent ones in the Jesus's parable and, as myself in the past, there are many today who feel overexposed to the world's pain, so they become disconnected, blind, and deaf. We are tempted to say that it is not our doing or responsibility, but someone else's. We have no time for it. Or, we react only when it hits home in our own lives. I guess I have answered my own question of why all these advanced human accomplishments have not taken care of the world's urgent needs: because they are not always managed by compassionate, burdened hearts. To make a difference, we need to share everything unconditionally and freely, to be willing to invest our own lives in the process of healing. Imagine the tremendous power and potential if together we could link the wealth of knowledge and resources of this day and age with the most compassionate givers and healers! Love and its fruit would find no limit. Those three groups of characters in the parable of the Good Samaritan will one day

1. Robert Rieth's Media Fellowship International luncheons in New York City were hosted by Michael P. Grace II.

> become two. The broken will be healed and become healers. There is no doubt in my mind that everyone can also be made to see with opening eyes, hearts, and arms those who are still in the gutter where they themselves were once found. And, when the question is asked, "Who gave me to eat when I was hungry and to drink when I was thirsty, and who visited me while sick and in prison?" (Matt 25:35-36), don't you want to hear your name announced, as the Lord, smiling at you, beckons you forward saying, "Come blessed of my Father?" This is the one calling that we all share in common, because ultimately sharing God's love with compassion will be the only thing that matters.[2]

In a recent interview, disabled veteran John Joseph DeFazio voiced concern about the physically and mentally ill homeless veteran population:

> As a disabled veteran with a service related back injury, I contacted Ted Puntillo, Yolo County Veteran's Service Officer and got help. I am contributing to this dialogue to encourage veterans who have service related physical or psychological illness to contact their County's Veterans Service Officer and get help!

In an interview this morning, Lori Chang, wife of Howard Chang, pastor of Davis Chinese Christian Church in Davis, California, explained:

> I suffered with anxiety and depression for years. I was encouraged to pray and read the Bible more, but my symptoms persisted. A therapist explained to me that the chemical imbalance in my brain causing the depression and anxiety is treatable with medication in the same way diabetes is treatable with insulin. I am leading a fuller happier life today after seeking professional help and want to encourage those with depression and anxiety to do the same.[3]

Howard and Lori Chang's daughter, Lydia, has a bipolar disorder. In her blog, *sincerely, Lydia*, she shares her healing experience. I want to close with this word of hope paraphrased from Lydia's post from September 12, 2018: "If you find out you have a bipolar disorder, you will learn how to live with it. Your cuts will become healed scars and you will reach those goals that slipped away from you."[4]

2. Martha Reyes, "Healing Through Faith and Compassion," in DeFazio and Spencer, eds., *Redeeming the Screens*, 94–95.

3. Lori Chang, interview in person, February 10, 2019.

4. Chang, "dear Lydia."

I want to encourage everyone to seek healing and restoration. Living with a condition will be challenging, but I have seen many people experience dramatic changes and live totally functional and prosperous lives.

If I can help you, contact me.

Martha Reyes
Email: Dr.MarthaReyes@aol.com

Preface

In 1986, Dorothy Frooks featured a front-page article in the *Murray Hill News* entitled "Her Dream Needs Realism." Dorothy's article identified Harriet Lorence Nesbitt as an artist, social activist, and aristocrat who had a dream.[1] It was Harriet's dream to sell her art to benefit mentally ill youth. January 29, 2019 was the first anniversary of Harriet's passing. The idea to publish a book of her art work was on my mind that day. I contacted her nephew, Michael Nesbitt (executor to the estate of Harriet Lorence Nesbitt), his wife, Martha, and was told that her son, New York attorney Roger Lorence, granted me permission to publish this collection of Harriet's artworks so that the proceeds of this book could benefit mentally ill youth. In this way her dream of helping mentally ill youth with her art will be realized.

Jeanne DeFazio

1. Frooks, "Her Dream Needs Realism."

Acknowledgments

THANK YOU TO DR. William David Spencer for reading the manuscript and making helpful suggestions. I would like to acknowledge Harriet Nesbitt's son, Roger Lorence, her nephew, Michael Nesbitt, and his wife, Martha, for supporting this project. Thanks to Taylor Cecil for help with formatting this book! Shaun Cass and Dillion Santos have been instrumental in the successful completion of this project! Thanks to my beautiful and wonderful niece, Ella Louise Ryan, for reminding me to prioritize health and wellbeing. Thanks to Michelle DeFazio, MLIS, for the sensitivity and care she gives the homeless and mentally ill patrons in the San Diego Public Library. Thanks to Gerald Anthony Maguire, MD, Gerald Eugene Maguire, MD, Louise Maguire, MSW, and clinical psychologist Michael Maguire—lifelong champions of mental health prevention, diagnosis, and treatment. Thanks to Governor Jerry Brown, who passed legislation for the state of California to provide parents, teachers, and schools with the tools they need to help save the lives of at-risk youth. Special thanks to Caleb Loring III for supporting this work. Remembering Davis, California police officer Natalie Corona for her courageous life and legacy! Most important, I thank Jesus!

JEANNE DEFAZIO

Reflections on the Art of Harriet Lorence Nesbitt

Jeanne DeFazio

Harriet Lorence Nesbitt was a wonderful friend. I am grateful to have known her and the many wonderful people I met and grew to love through her. We talked often in the thirty-plus years of our friendship. Her clever and funny comments on life and broadcast journalism in particular still speak to me. She searched for order and meaning in life as an artist, as founder of Mothers for More Halfway Houses, at the death of her son Larry, and as *Murray Hill News*'s "Politics and Such" columnist. Olga Soler's book *Apocalypse of Youth* reflects on the matters of social significance Harriet addressed in "Politics and Such." I recommend readers go on Amazon and read Olga's book to understand Harriet's concern about the environment, the AIDs epidemic, racial issues, and the dangers of artificial intelligence. Her words of wisdom speak to the challenges of our time. In the back cover endorsement of Olga Soler's *Apocalypse of Youth*, I explained: "Harriet Nesbitt is a level headed and rare find in a partisan and polarizing world. If more eyes were like hers to see things as they are, and more ears as well to listen to the pleas of those in need, we might have understanding and productive compromise. Even as an elder she intrepidly approaches the giants of society as equals with her art . . . forcing all of us . . . to think."

Tickertape

New York is famous for parades and Charles Lindbergh's and John Glenn's were two of New York's finest. Harriet depicted both in this diptych and the hailstorm of confetti and celebrities that went with them, as Jay Maeder explains:

> *In 1927 Col. Charles Lindbergh become the most famous man on Earth for this epic solo flight around the earth . . . He soared into history and was accompanied by an honor guard of 21 Army planes to New York City and* Lindbergh received the greatest salute the city had ever witnessed . . . Four million people screamed welcome from the streets and building tops as Lindbergh's motorcade inched through a blinding confetti snowstorm, from the Battery up lower Broadway to City Hall Plaza . . . You can hear the heartbeats of 6 million people," said Mayor Jimmy Walker, pinning a medal on Lindbergh's chest. "And the story they tell is one of pride and one of admiration. As you went over the ocean, you inscribed on the heavens themselves a beautiful rainbow of hope and courage and confidence in mankind. Col. Lindbergh, New York City is yours. I don't give it to you. You won it.[1]

Patrick Healy notes of Glenn:

> It is March 1, 1962. There is bright sunshine across Lower Manhattan, and a crowd is building. New Yorkers still love a parade. The ritual of throwing blizzards of ticker tape from the windows of stock brokerages has become a cherished tradition. People are lining the sidewalks of Broadway, two deep, then four deep, then six deep. And they keep arriving . . . they are waiting to see the most famous man in America that day. As many as four million people turned out that morning to celebrate Lt. Col. John H. Glenn Jr., who had become the first American to orbit the Earth only nine days earlier. For a nation rattled by the Soviet Union's advances in space, including putting a man in orbit the year before, the Ohioan radiated the can-do attitude, frontier spirit and gusty valor that characterized the best of his countrymen.[2]

As I read these words, I am reminded of how Harriet often told me why Lindbergh personified the American dream for his generation. Raymond Orteig, the owner of New York City's Hotel Lafayette, envisioned the day

1. Maeder, "Day New York City Threw."
2. Healy, "For John Glenn."

when the United States and France would be linked by aviation. He offered $25,000 to the first pilot who could fly nonstop between New York and Paris.[3] Lindbergh in 1927 become the most famous man on Earth after his epic solo flight on the *Spirit of St. Louis* from New York to Paris. *Tickertape* lets viewers experience the thrill of the crowds screaming welcome to the hero and celebrities traveling through a blinding confetti snowstorm from the Battery up lower Broadway to City Hall Plaza. As she said, Lindbergh was a Midwestern boy who made good.

In 1962, Lt. Col. John H. Glenn Jr. became the first American to orbit the Earth. *Tickertape* demonstrates the excitement and pride the most famous man in America caused by advancing the US in its fierce competition with the USSR to win the race to conquer outer space. What made this event so fantastic in Harriet's understanding was the fact that it was televised globally as a triumph of American ingenuity and the bravery of another Midwesterner. Harriet composed the two events as a diptych to honor Lindbergh and Glenn for demonstrating true grit as American superheroes.

3. Learning Network, "Charles Lindbergh Flies Solo," lines 72–74.

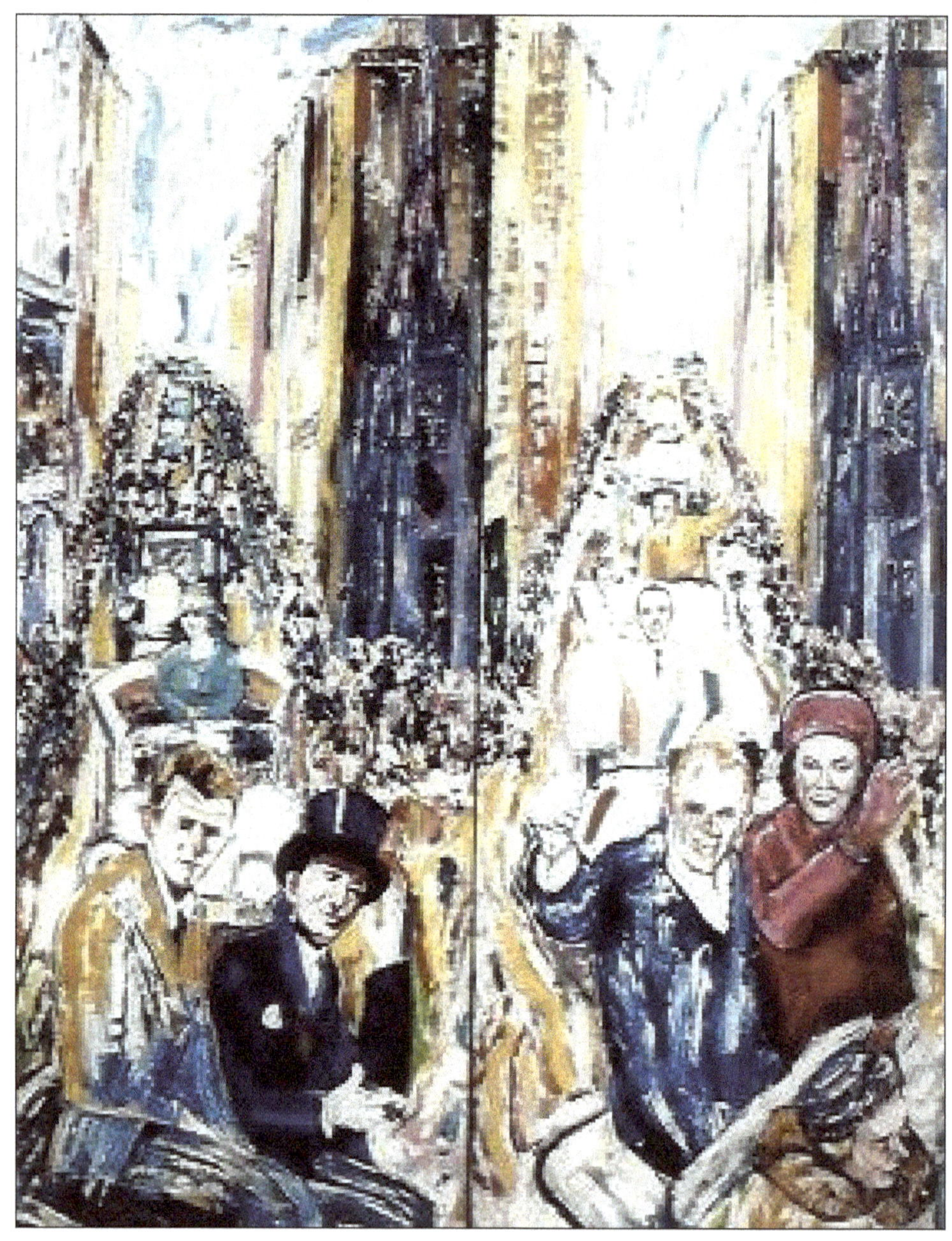

Symphony Americana[1]

Contrast and congestion punctuate Harriet's artistic commentary. Harriet's *Symphony Americana* features Van Cliburn as the most prominent figure in the composition. The symphony of the industrialized dreams of music produces cacophony or harmony. She painted *Symphony Americana* because she believed that Van Cliburn's Russian concerts eased tensions between the Soviet Union and the United States during the Cold War. "*Symphony Americana* demonstrates the creative power of art to unite humankind."[2] *Symphony Americana* was displayed at the 1964 opening of the Newark, New Jersey Arts Center.

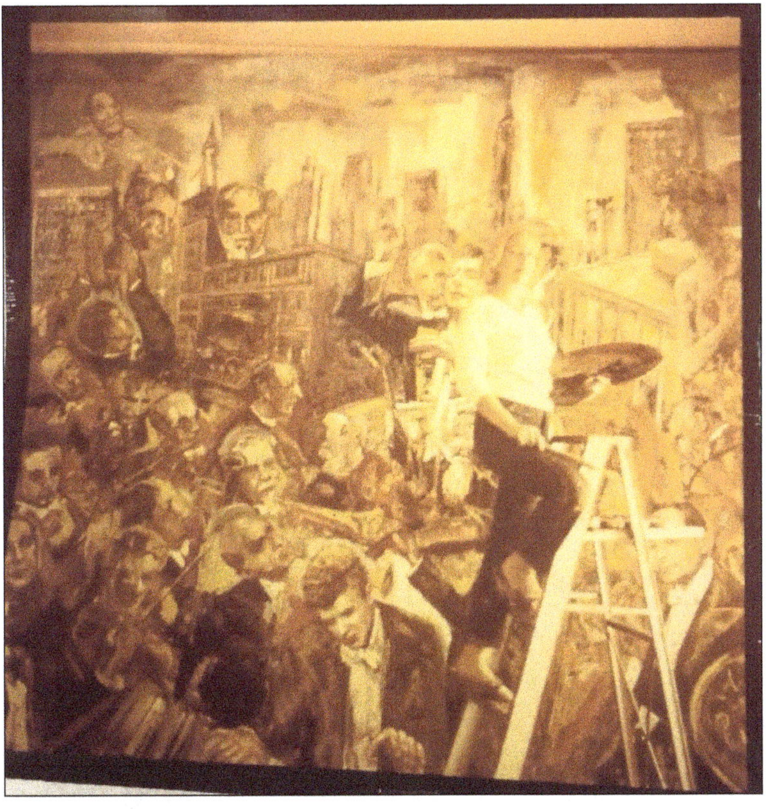

1. The young Harriet Lorence Nesbitt on a ladder in front of *Symphony Americana*.
2. Madigan, "Van Cliburn."

The Kennedy Family Diptych: Panel One

Harriett like so many others considered the Kennedy family the epitome of magnanimity. She took this to iconic proportion in her artwork depicting the assassinated president in saintly white garb and his family surrounded by light couched in the stained glass windows of an ethereal cathedral. Both Kennedy brothers were featured in her work as modern martyrs for the cause of justice.

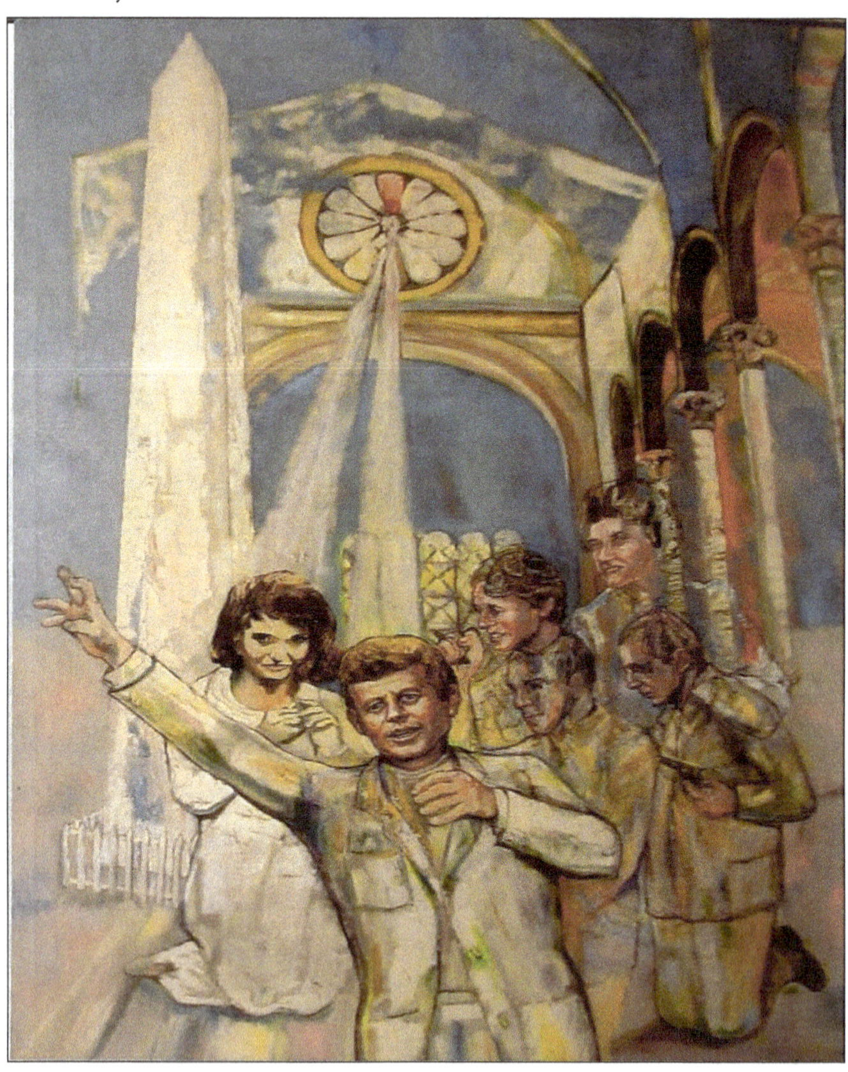

The Kennedy Family Diptych: Panel Two

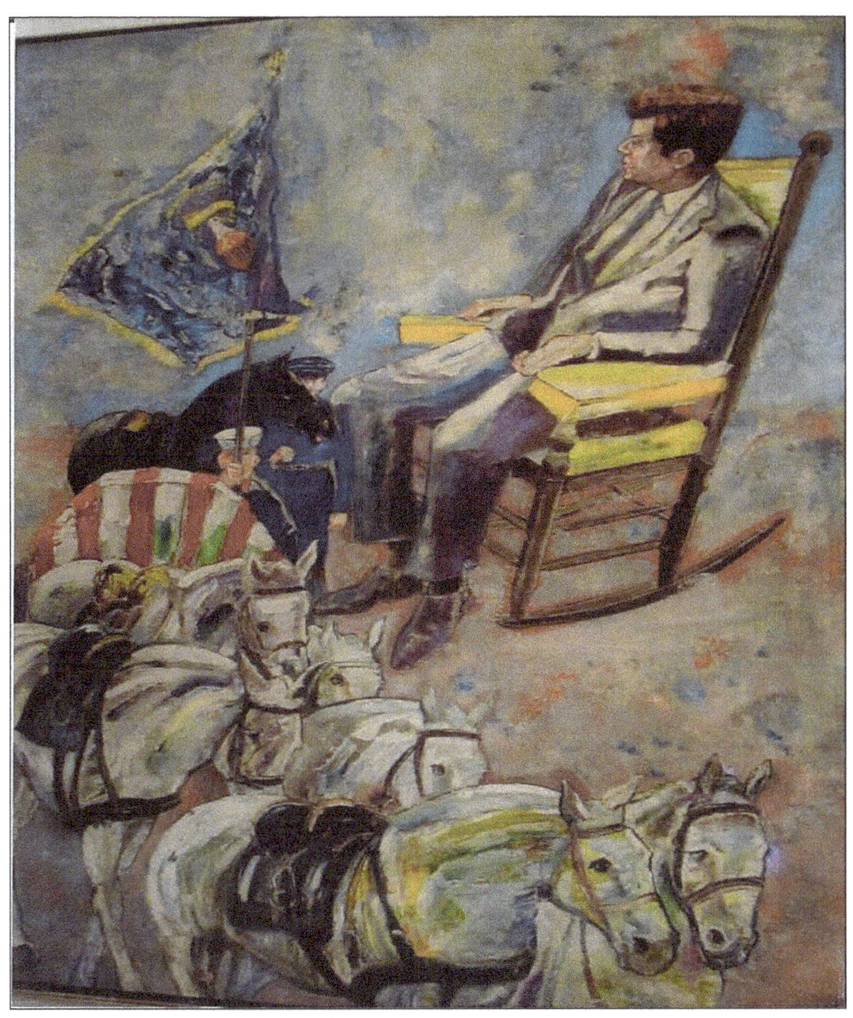

Apocalypse of Youth

As Picasso exemplified all the horrors of war in one mural he christened *Guernica*, so Harriet in her *Apocalypse* illustrates succinctly the thousands of conflicts facing the young by one who has survived the maelstrom of social change in the last eighty years.[1]

Here is Harriet's reflection:

> *Apocalypse of Youth* is my artistic comment on the pitfalls of youth in a millennial society. It is a collage of imagery which include a Rolls Royce, the closing of New York City's 68th Street baby orphanage, John the Divine's four horsemen of the apocalypse from the Book of Revelation, a scene from the epic disaster Three Mile Island, planes dropping bombs, Jesus and Mary blessing youth, a student with a blue Three Mile Island sweater riding a red demonic horse next to a boy on a horse. [2]

In *Apocalypse of Youth*, Harriet expressed heartache at losing her son Larry. It was the crisis that put her life in order to reach out and help other mentally ill youth:

> Dr. Pangloss, the eternal optimist in Voltaire's satire *Candide*, believed that in spite of everything it is the best of all possible worlds. I believe that every challenge provides an open door. My son Larry died tragically and at his death I founded Mothers for More Halfway Houses so that those struggling with mental illness have shelter to heal. Meeting Mother Teresa inspired me to continue work as founder of MMHH. In conclusion I want to remind readers of her words: *At the hour of death we are going to be judged on what we have been to the poor, to the hungry, naked, the homeless, and he (Jesus) makes himself that hungry one, that naked one, that homeless one, not only hungry for bread, but hungry for love, not only naked for a piece of cloth, but naked of that human dignity, not only homeless for a room to live, but homeless for that being forgotten, being unloved, uncared, being nobody to nobody, having forgotten what is human love, what is human touch, what is to be loved by somebody, and he says: Whatever you did to the least of these my brethren, you did it to me.* Mother Teresa ended her speech quoting Jesus: *Whatever you did to the least of these my brethren, you did it to me.* My son Larry, like Mother Teresa, understood the

1. Soler, *Apocalypse of Youth*, ix.
2. Soler, *Apocalypse of Youth*, xii.

> importance of spiritual guidance. He left me his Bible and in times of discouragement and, when I still miss him more than I can bear, I open it as a point of contact. I feel Larry's presence every day and especially when I am in contact with my son Roger. Larry Nesbitt did not die in vain. His memory lives on through this work.[3]

Harriet became closer to God as she struggled through grief and loss. In her final years, she had a close call with death. She described her heart failing and the way she called out to Jesus for help and in an instant recovered. From that time on, she let me know that she, like our mutual friend, Michael P Grace II, was a born-again Christian and that Jesus was her Lord and Savior. She prayed with me often toward the end, understanding that her time was short and that she wanted to be with Jesus and the angels when she left this Earth. She still had unrealized dreams, but she was secure in the love of Jesus for all eternity.

Harriet's journey of artistic expression and how she met the challenge and devastation of her son's untimely death by helping others and, in her frail last years, by her embracing of Jesus as Lord and Savior, together speak to us all.

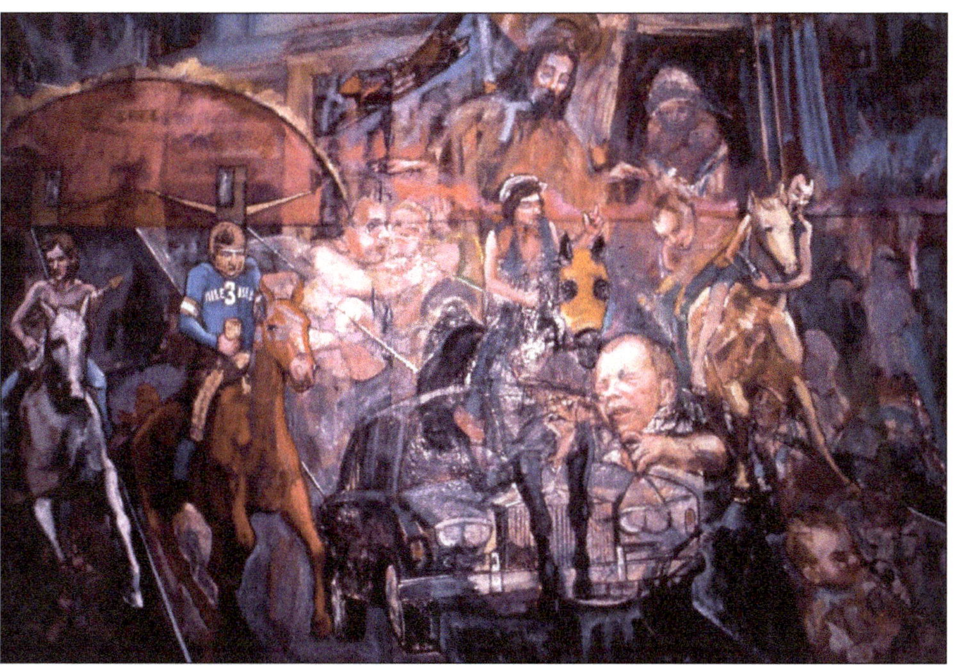

3. Soler, *Apocalypse of Youth*, 59–62.

Sandy the Storm

Nothing left but a porch! Disaster impressed her, in particular Hurricane Sandy, which left one couple nothing but their porch, an image of Sandy's trail of destruction. Hurricane Sandy, a late-season post-tropical cyclone, swept through the Caribbean and up the East Coast of the United States in late October 2012. The storm left dozens dead, thousands homeless, and millions without power. Total damage was in the billions of dollars.[1] *Sandy the Storm* received a California Motion Picture Council Award for artistic excellence in Hollywood California on December 16, 2013. Harriet's painting focused on an New York City couple who had nothing left but a porch. Harriet completed *Sandy the Storm* to show concern for the devastating impact of climate change.

1. Walsh, "Frankenstorm."

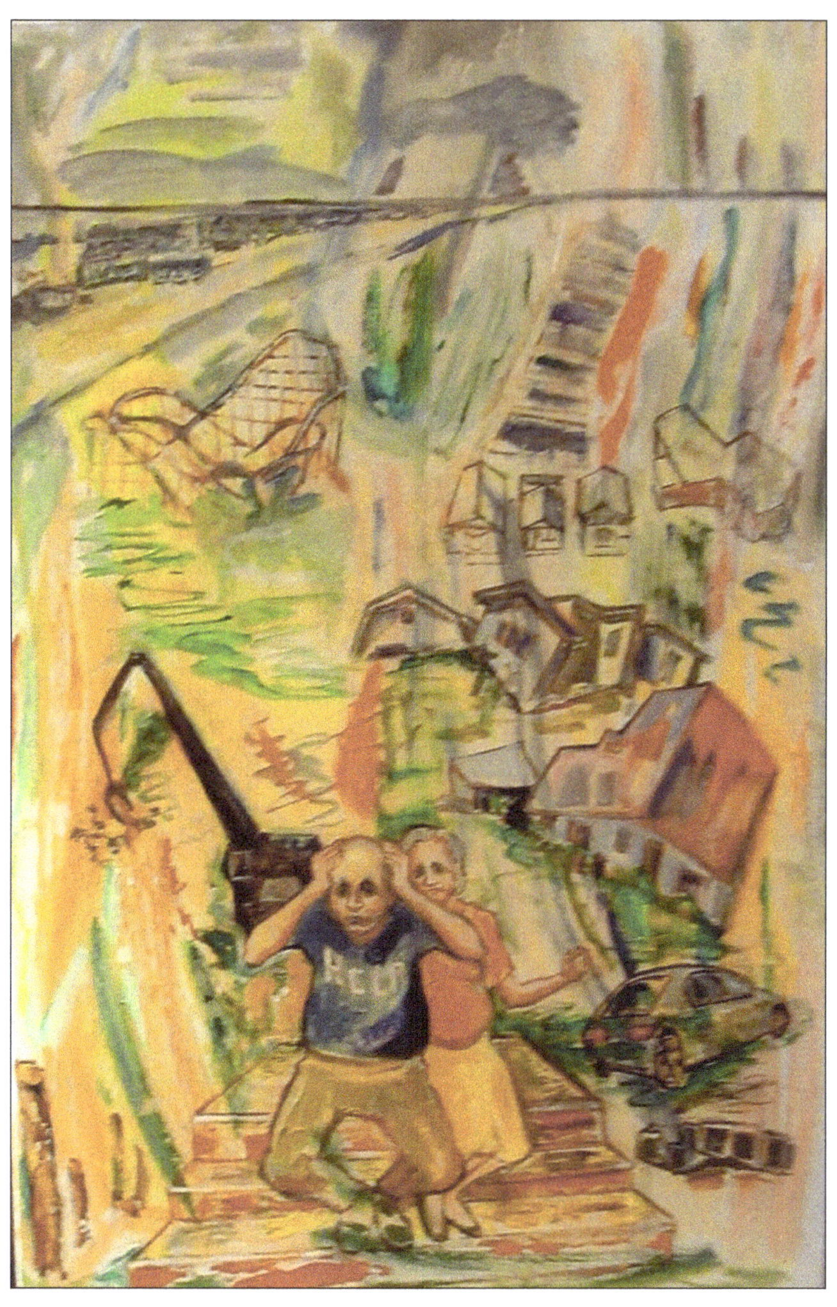

Mayor Koch

Mayor Koch of New York was not just a statesman but a showman, poignant, good-natured, straightforward, and humorous. He is depicted here with two arches behind him of windows that look like wings. Angel, comedian, and all-American—Mayor Koch. The La Guardia Wagner Archives selected Nesbitt's portrait of Mayor Ed Koch as a permanent part of the La Guardia Wagner Collection.[1]

Harriet loved Mayor Koch's sense of self. In his own words: "I know that nothing happens here on this Earth that wasn't ordained by God. I know that. You know that. And therefore, while I know that it was the people who elected me, it was God who selected me. Not that I was given approval by the Deity, but I am delighted I was given the opportunity by the Deity."[2] Harriet liked the fact that Koch knew that nothing happens here on this Earth that wasn't ordained by God. She emphasized that Koch knew it was the people who elected him but God who selected him. Koch was, to Harriet's mind, New York City's guardian angel.

1. Permission to publish this digital image granted by the La Guardia and Wagner Archives, La Guardia Community College/City University of New York. https://www.ny.com/museums/lwarchives.html. Special thanks to Douglas DiCarlo.

2. "Best Ed Koch Quotes."

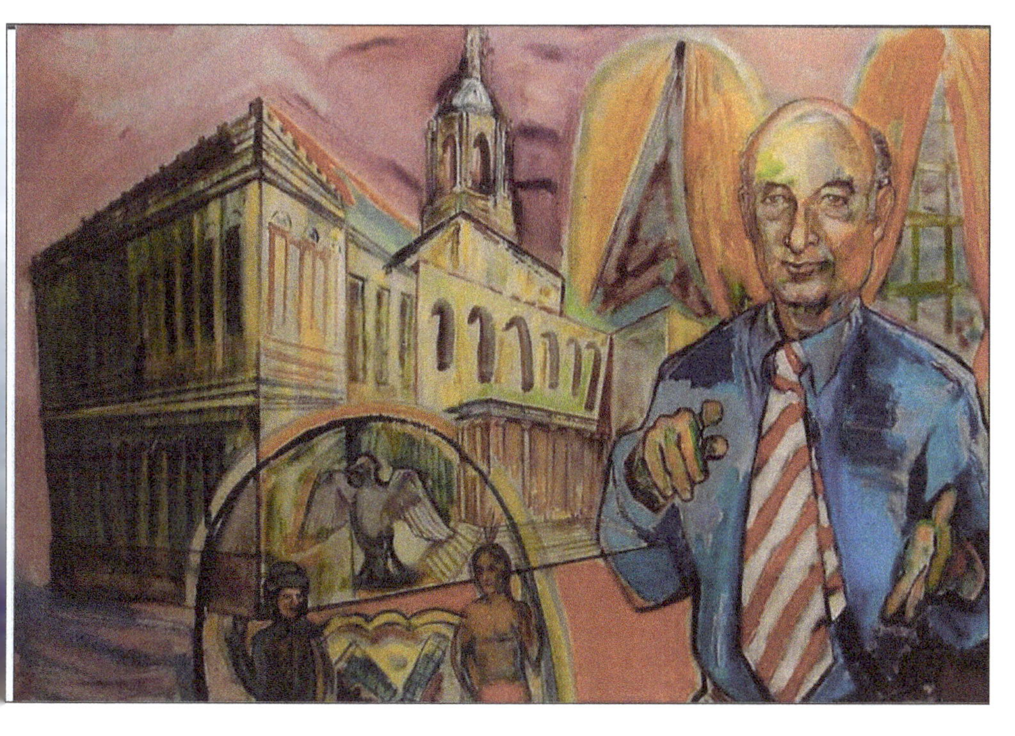

The Breadline

The Breadline has the somber tones of a Goya chiaroscuro and insight into the extent of poverty as a line drifting into an endless horizon. Harriett believed, as do so many others, that poverty is something perennial that would always be with us, but she applauded those with means who tried to ameliorate it in any way possible.

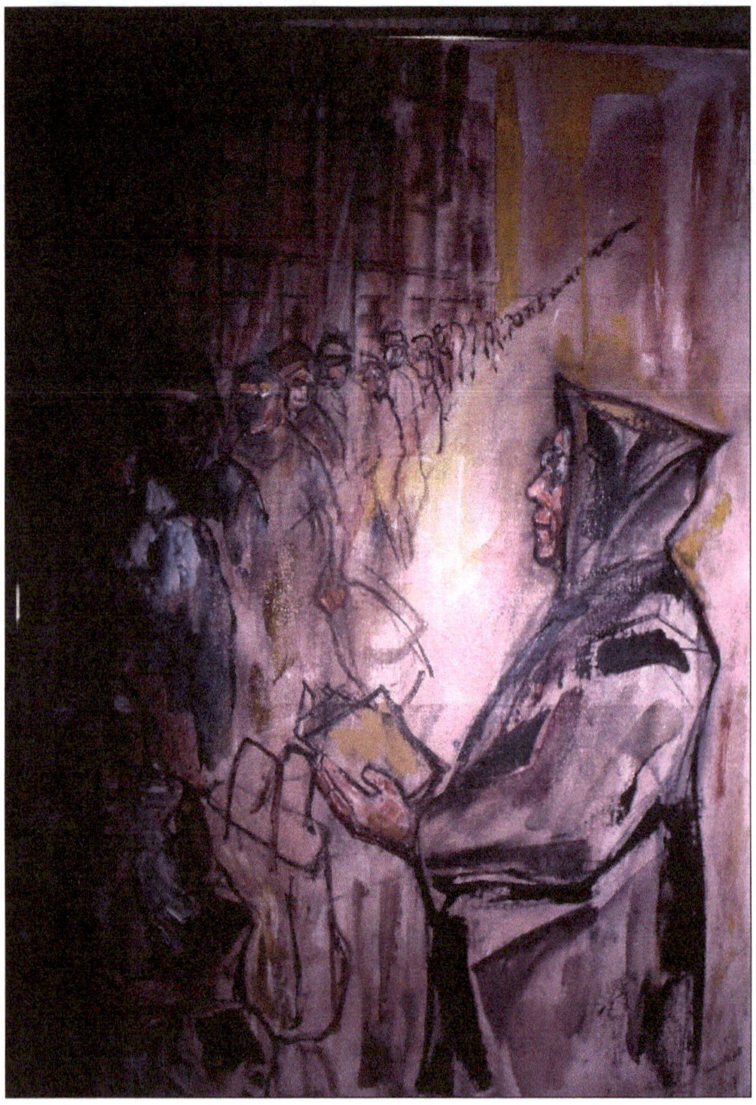

Scrooge Vann Rye Neck

Harriet's *Scrooge Vann Rye Neck* is the modern-day counterpart of Dicken's classic *Christmas Carol* villain: greedy, selfish, and lacking in mercy toward the destitute.[1] Bob Cratchit carrying Tiny Tim are likenesses of Harriet's husband, Dick Nesbitt, and her son, Larry Nesbitt. Harriet wanted at the close of her life to paint *The Haves and Have Nots*. She was not able to do so because she was too frail. It clearly hurt her heart, even as a child of privilege, that society so easily showed contempt for the destitute. She often paraphrased Mahatma Ghandi by saying that our society will be judged by the way we treat the most vulnerable.

1. Priestley, "Ignorance and Want."

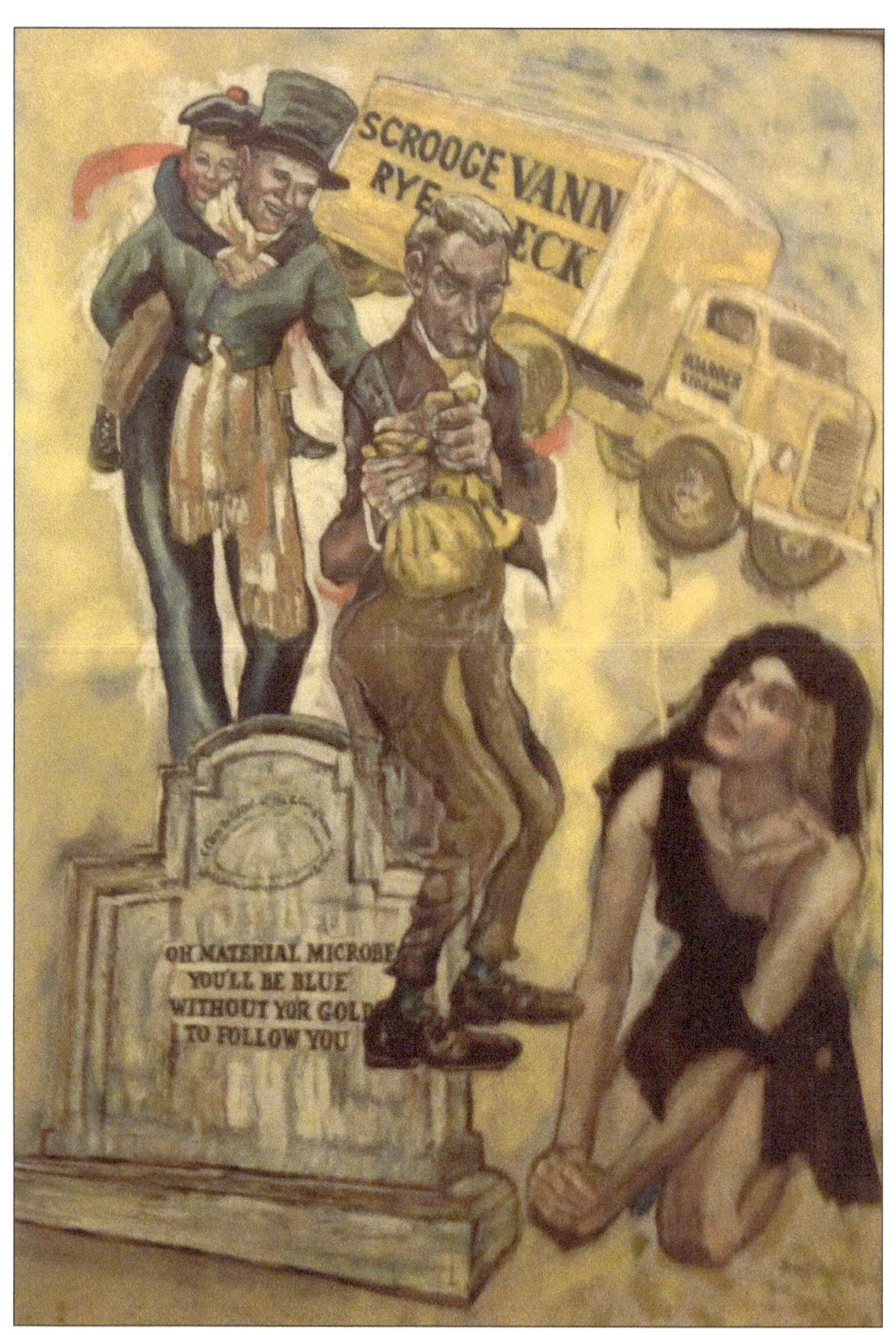
SCROOGE VANN
RYE ECK
OH MATERIAL MICROBE
YOU'LL BE BLUE
WITHOUT YOR GOLD
TO FOLLOW YOU

Horse Paintings

A great theme of Harriet's art was the racehorse or more specifically the horse races. These paintings were her most popular and they are in the collections of prominent individuals. The dust and drama of these thundering specimens, with their brightly colored riders vying for preeminence at dizzying speeds and sometimes colliding, became her most popular and prolific works.

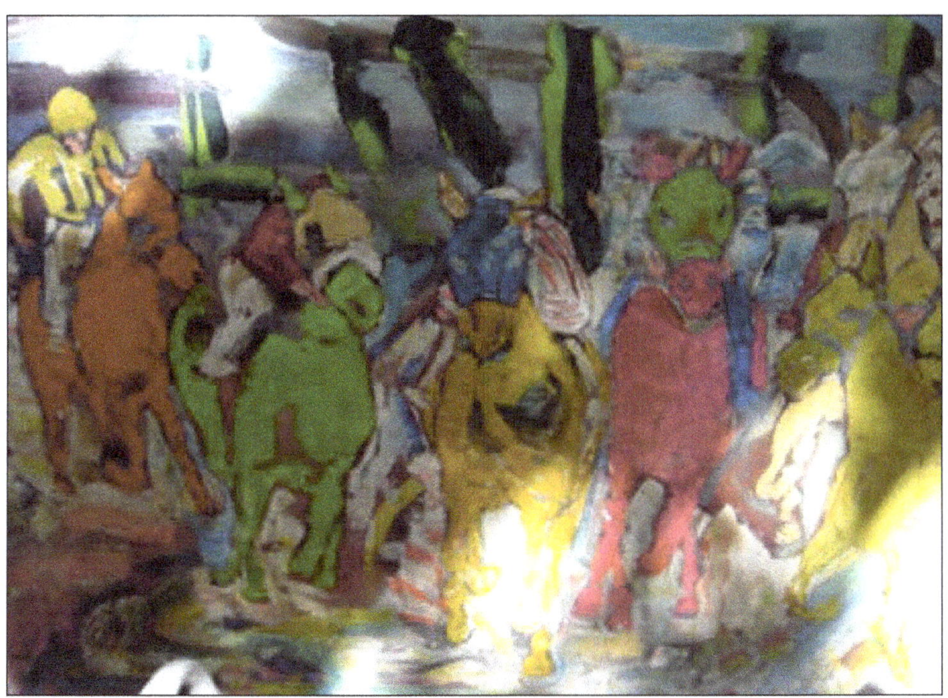

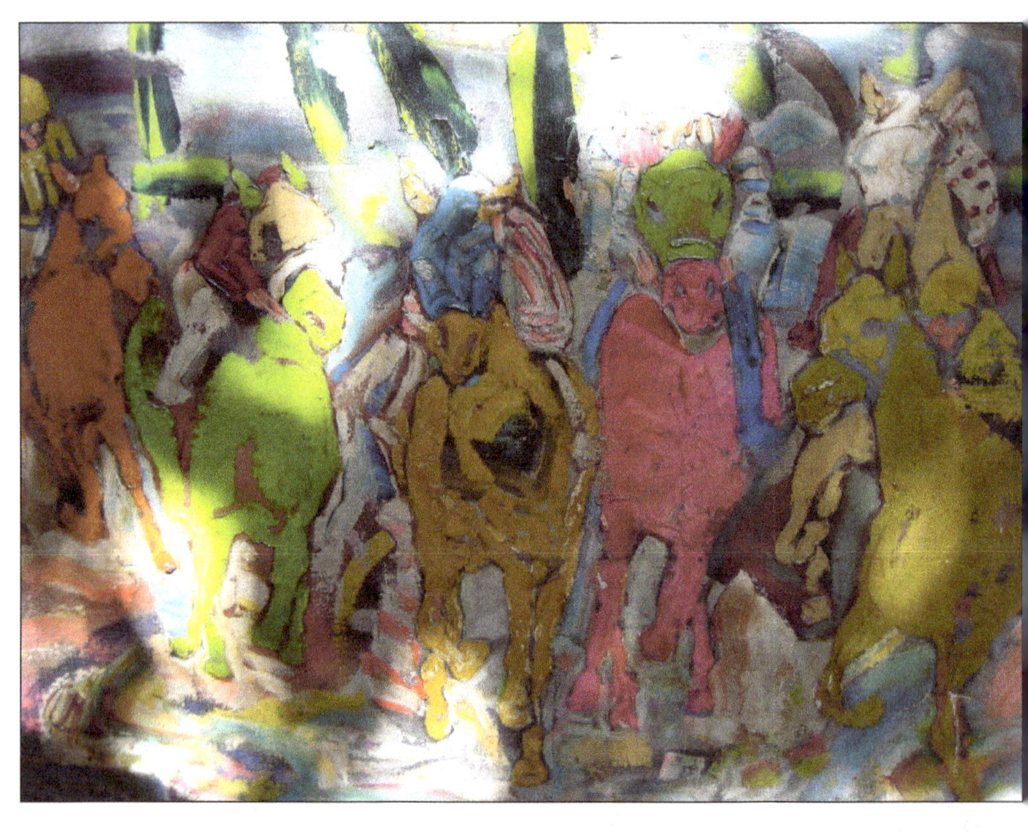

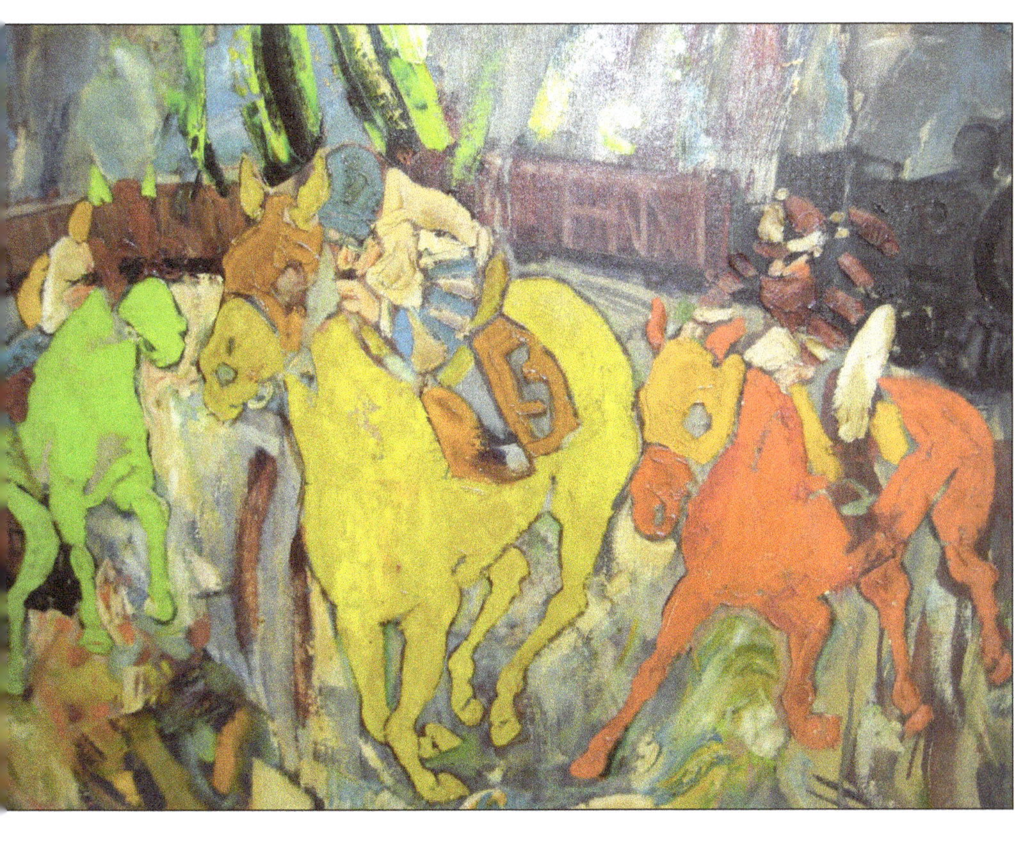

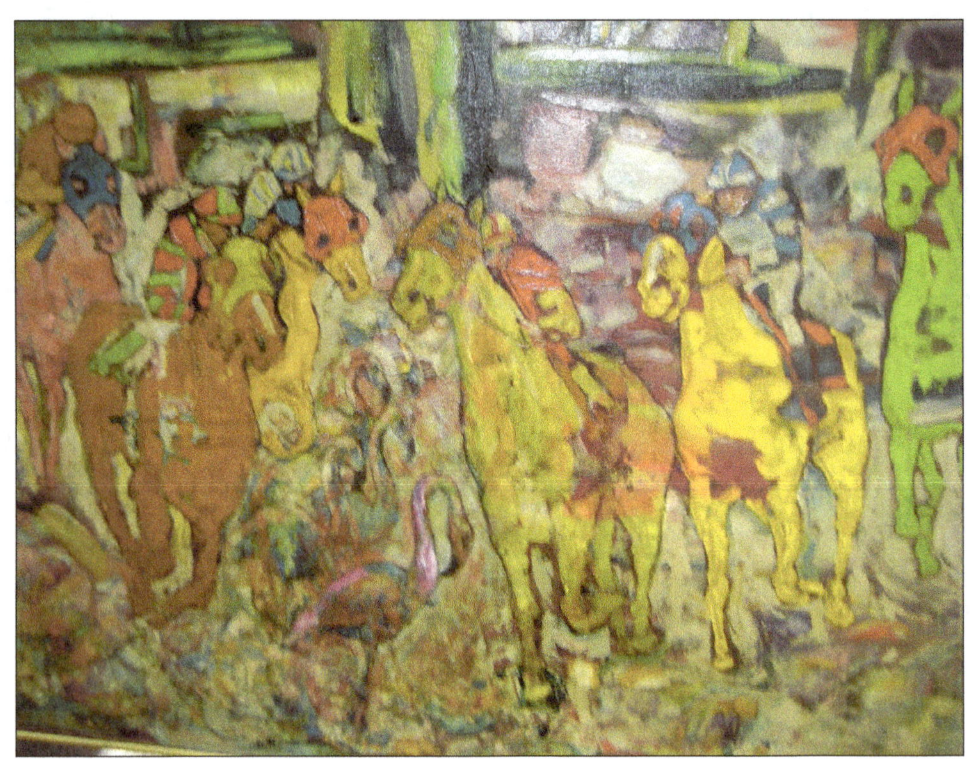

The Atomic Madonna

My favorite times with Harriet were going to the Metropolitan Museum of Art. She knew every painting. Bellini's *Madonna and Child* inspired her to create *The Atomic Madonna*. It is a self-portrait of Harriet and her son Larry. The contrast of the Prince of Peace and his mother with the nuclear mushroom cloud in the background depicts her concern for the danger of nuclear war and annihilation.

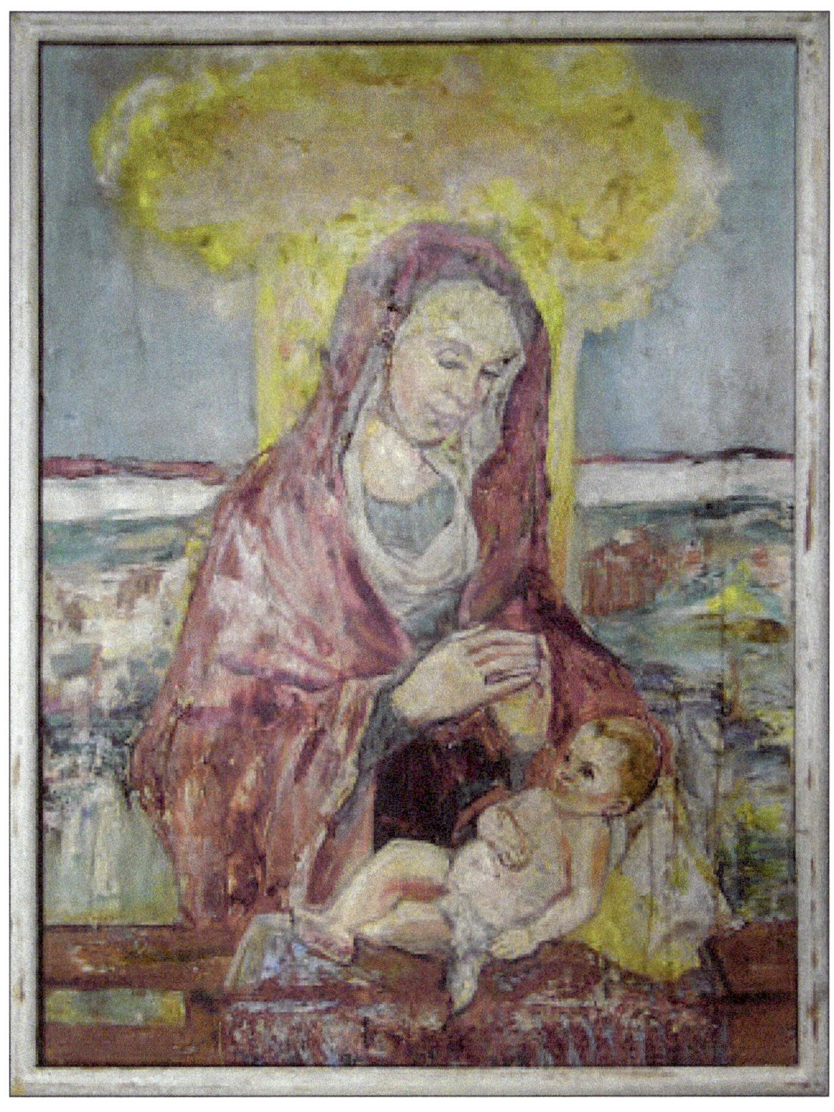

Afterword

William David Spencer

The paintings of Harriet Lorence Nesbitt pulse with vibrancy that strikes a new viewer immediately. So much is happening before you that taking each in often seems overwhelming. Her work is not Jackson Pollack's. It is far from abstract expressionism. Though it is emotive like Pollack's "snowstorms," yet it is representational. But, at the same time, her work is not representational with the precision of an Andrew Wyeth, though, as his work does, hers aims at creating a mood for viewers. Her art, I think, blossoms somewhere in the vast terrain between these two, though both artists were her contemporaries. To my eye, her sensibility seems to be closer to that of Paul Gauguin in the kind of design and active element she invests in her human figures, though she and Gauguin were from another age, another time, another choice of subjects and settings. As a contemporary, she does share with Pollack a sense of action in her art, but those emotions are driven by a message that demands a representational value and conduit, one approaching but stopping far short of the way Wyeth builds mood into his careful depictions. What I am noticing is that Harriet is all about the action, but an action rooted in events, and the subjects she chooses to paint are portrayed as active in these events, each as a synecdoche to the kind of impact on the viewer her vision demands.

Arguably, each of these remarkable artists I have mentioned thus far has used technique to reveal something about each one's understanding of the meaning of life. Harriet's expression in her art is often invested in figures who drive events, and with these she fills her backgrounds with the sketchy suggestion of others they impact. And this, to my eye, is what makes her work distinctive. But she can also concentrate on portraying the victims, as she does in *Scrooge*, *Sandy the Storm*, and *Breadline*, and in these evil looms around them and their dismay is emotive and palpable. They beg the viewer to provide succor.

We should also note that Harriet's paintings locate not on the land, as the bulk and best of Andrew Wyeth's, or in the emotions, as Pollack's, but in the city. And the topics they express have to do with people and events that concern multitudes rather than individuals or an artist's inner emotions. It might not be inaccurate to call her an urban critic for the players in her best-known pictures are urban active: New York's Mayor Koch, President John F. Kennedy, aviator Charles Lindbergh and astronaut John Glenn, President Barak Obama, and others, each being depicted in settings that link them with the environments in which they are celebrated for their impact on others.

For example, Harriet depicts neither Charles Lindbergh nor John Glenn in the sky or in outer space, where their triumphs took place, but juxtaposed in parades, presumably down New York's Wall Street, the center of finance and business. In the left-hand side of *Tickertape*, only the three figures of Charles Lindbergh, host, Jimmy Walker, and a woman seated behind them are distinct; the rest are in relief, just suggestions of figures. Lindbergh is depicted as serious, tight-lipped, showing the iron resolve of a man whose irresistible will is able both to challenge death and triumph, single-handedly lifting the spirits of a nation, but also able to embrace fascism and alarm the same nation. New York Mayor Jimmy Walker in his high hat appears to my eye as a veteran of many such celebrations, leaning back to gage the effect on his crowd of constituents. John Glenn, on the right side of the diptych, is another story entirely: relaxed, smiling, sharing the space with five figures made distinct, a hero enjoying the moment among family and fans. In *Symphony Americana*, the setting is all action and all intensely crowded. Pianist Van Cliburn is hard at work at the bottom, front center, pressed in by an orchestra, a set of buildings against an industrial sky, and influential faces watching. He leads the musicians with total concentration on his own contribution to the harmony of the whole, spurring them on by model. This painting too is crowded, busy, even claustrophobic, and, to my mind, extremely effective. I think it is my favorite in her remarkable work.

An undeniable political dimension typifies her choice of subjects. None of her politicians, including Barak Obama, seem by her to be ordinarily presented in repose or reflection. In *The Kennedy Family* diptych's first representation, John Kennedy still appears to me to be orating though dead (although others may read his posture differently) as his wife and other significant family members kneel behind him, and only as he contemplates his funeral in the second panel of *The Kennedy Family* his funeral is he relaxed in a rocking chair, the symbol of final repose. Otherwise, the settings and the figures they frame are all active. Mayor Koch, for example, gestures before the seal and center of his legacy. So Harriet Nesbitt's interest often concentrated on what are popularly called the movers and shakers, the active drivers of terrestrial events. At the same time, she became aware of the impact of the celestial, as in her *Atomic Madonna* painting of Mary praying with the peace that passes all understanding over Jesus as the detonated atomic mushroom cloud festoons amidst a set of buildings behind her, indicating why we need so desperately the Prince of Peace.

Also worthy to note is the cartoonish quality about the way she sometimes presents her subjects, a distinguishing element about her pictures that makes them identifiable. This approach suggests she could have had a stellar career as an adroit and successful syndicated purveyor of political cartoons. She did serve the *Murry Hill News* with the column "Politics and Such." Or, given her talents and interests and the greater flexibility of genres now available, one might wonder: If Harriet Nesbitt were a young art student starting out today, would she be tempted to write a graphic novel? Full of political opinions and artfully presented, the graphic novel earned profound respect in 1992 when *Maus*, a "graphic memoir" of the Holocaust, told through the vehicle of a paneled art cat-and-mouse tale, won the Pulitzer Prize's "Special Award in Letters," as well as the American Book Award.[1] In her youth, however, the comic book had little if any artistic regard. If she were born and reared even more recently in our present globally oriented, popular artistic culture, however, would she have been captured by the often dense, frequently urban oriented, and politically charged melding of artful animation with emotional dimensions that has developed from Japanese manga, the traditional picture-book style, infused by the invasion of United States' cartooning during the occupation (1945–52), which hyperspaced globally in the wake of Osamu Tezuka's *Mighty Atom* (serialized in *Shonen Magazine*, 1952–1968, and known globally as *Astro Boy*)? Harriet Nesbitt, of course, was alive to witness all this and her own paintings of horses do portray the high-energy quality of the best of Japanese manga and would certainly lend themselves to manga, the story books, and anime,

1. See, for example, Cavna, "Why 'Maus' Remains 'the Greatest Graphic Novel.'"

Japanese animated films.[2] Only ten years old in 1938[3] (the year the Second World War began in earnest and DC first presented Superman to little artistic acclaim), she was thirty three and already forging a different path by 1961 when the maturation of Marvel[4] was graphically counterbalancing the DC type of superhero with a kind of surreal, animated quality that suggests the characterizations of Harriet's own kind of impressionistic adaptions. The postwar years were also the period of the blossoming of manga, but her vision was set on depicting, not fantasy, but real stories about real human heroes. Her vision directed her to depict particular scenes in the lives of specific people she found interesting because of their authentic accomplishments in the real world. In this way, she served as a kind of human pictorial reporter, catching her subjects in significant moments that framed and, thereby, furthered her vision of how people should act to bring about how life should be.

Where we might observe that Gauguin took great pains to travel to Tahiti and the Marquesas Islands to find the exotic, Harriet Nesbitt recognized the exotic in life around her. Wild nature is captured in her renderings of galloping horses that race through several exciting paintings where jockeys crouch and dust swirls up, as horses veer to the right or charge straight on through all the bewildering pastimes, pressures, and temptations of her *Apocalypse of Youth*. Yet, for all her horses wildness, she still has contained these animals mainly in a race, an event that could easily figure into a 1930s–40s film noir mystery wherein the urbane William Powell and Myrna Loy could be enjoying the melee from a private box, sipping something alcoholic, winning wagers, and solving stylized murders. So, even nature in her vision is funneled through its impact on people, those invested (sometimes to desperation) in a civilized derby or steeple chase event, or victimized in the visceral calamities of life, as in her depiction of *Sandy the Storm*, wherein an astonished husband and wife, seated helplessly amidst

2. See *Widewalls Magazine's* editorial "A Short History of Japanese Manga," on manga, the story books, and anime, the term usually applied to the animated films. The term "manga" was first applied to a picture book by Santō Kyōden in 1798, drawing on earlier tradition but flourishing in the late twentieth century to become the worldwide phenomenon it is today.

3. August 1, 1938, *Action Comics*, issue 1. See Wikipedia's entry for "Superman."

4. Though Stan Lee had been working since 1939 with Timely, he launched his first creation, The Fantastic Four, with Jack Kirby in 1961, eventually helping the company to become Marvel and both refurbish older heroes (e.g. Captain Marvel, who first appeared in *Whiz Comics* issue 2 [February 1940]) and create new ones (e.g., X-Men). See "Stan Lee Biography" and Kleefeld, "Where Does 'Marvel Comics' Come From?"

representative depictions of the extent of the ruin about them, gaze with despair into the miserific vision such a disaster reveals.

For this painting, on December 16, 2013, Harriet Nesbitt was honored by the Southern California Motion Picture Council with its Golden Halo Award. Vice President Bee Beyer in presenting the award announced, "This evening, the Motion Picture Council awarded Harriet Lorence Nesbitt's painting *Sandy the Storm* for artistic excellence. *Sandy the Storm* visually illustrates the conviction that drawing on God's grace in a natural disaster creates a mutually supportive human community. This poignant work of art highlights the values for which the SCMPC has stood unwaveringly since 1936: to produce art that is civic minded, educational, cultural and family oriented. Through the twin media of film and visual art, *Sandy the Storm* and the SCMPC partner to make a difference in this world."

Harriet Nesbitt replied, "I am thankful to the Motion Picture Council for giving my painting *Sandy the Storm* the Golden Halo Award for artistic excellence . . . Most of all I am thankful to those present here today who are sympathetic to the suffering of others and take action to make a difference."[5]

Like Bee Beyer, Harriet too had begun "drawing on God's grace" to combat disasters both personal and communal. For her, by this time, Jesus Christ had become more than simply the Christmas baby in the obscure manger; he and his mother were now personal. She modeled Mary on herself and the baby on her departed son. As the center of hope in a world gone awry, Jesus, the promise of grace, embodied the hope of reconciling humanity to the redeeming God, as he was given as God's gift to lead and inspire us all to do works of mercy and reconciliation. God had graced Earth with the greatest of all reformers, whose selfless sacrifice on behalf of humanity struck at the mushrooming symbol of the evil which is itself the root of human misery and suffering, as she depicted in her *Atomic Madonna*. The result united both Harriet and the Southern California Motion Picture Council in their agreement that disaster demands human response, drawing on God's grace for empowerment and modeling on Christ's example to do what we can to help alleviate suffering around us, even as God works through our good acts to reconcile this fallen world to Godself.

Had Harriet Nesbitt painted her vision-driven works in the late nineteenth century, she might have been called a "realist," as opposed to a naturalist. For, in her works, like *Sandy the Storm* and *The Atomic Madonna*, she is telling her viewers that overpowering nature or warmongers might seek to rule and destroy humanity, but the calling of humans who want to live

5. Jeanne DeFazio, interview by email, April 30, 2019.

significant lives is not to give in to them, but to prepare and oppose them and combat their threats by protecting civilization, as represented by her ever-present settings of urban scenes, for the city is where people gather for community, interconnection, and safe living. Each of the famous people she painted and the events she chose for their depiction can be seen as conveying this message: As aviators like Lindbergh and Glenn work to advance science, politicians to protect and advance civilization, musicians to sponsor harmony, the task of all human leaders is to bring about positive change by addressing challenging events that would disrupt such forward progress in each of their spheres, and accordingly receive well-earned honor for their triumphs. In her vision, that is the task of leaders: to tame natural forces and negative influences to bring under control a good government for the population that trusts these leaders. In short, to combat and conquer all threatening chaos to restore order, an order that takes into account a wide variety of recipients and provides a freer form for all its inhabitants than merely making cartographic map lines to demarcate turf and territory, such as fascism grants.

So strong was this vision and her identification with the efficacy of God's grace that she created a microcosmic parallel to the macrocosmic sacrifice of Jesus by infusing a corresponding redemptive dimension into the death of her younger son. To do this she stepped from the realm of art, fulfilling her identification with Mary in *The Atomic Madonna*, by becoming herself what she had admired in others, an active reformer. She created her own organization, as founder of Mothers for More Halfway Houses, explaining to her LinkedIn audience, "I am an advocate for the mentally ill, an artist as well as a political columnist."[6] She could not have expressed her vision more clearly by word or action. She had become one of her own subjects, what she admired most in those heroes she painted. She was now herself a leader in bringing positive order to the threatened lives of others in the real world as an agent of reconciliation of the Great Reconciler to this fallen world.

6. https://www.linkedin.com/in/harriet-nesbitt-1068a35a. Accessed March 12, 2019.

Bibliography

"Best Ed Koch Quotes." *New York Post*, February 1, 2013. https://nypost.com/2013/02/01/best-ed-koch-quotes/, https://nypost.com/2013/02/01/best-ed-koch-quotes/.

"Cavna, Michael. "Why 'Maus' Remains 'the Greatest Graphic Novel Ever Written,' 30 Years Later." *Washington Post*, August 11, 2016. https://www.washingtonpost.com/news/comic-riffs/wp/2016/08/11/why-maus-remains-the-greatest-graphic-novel-ever-written-30-years-later/?noredirect=on&utm_term=.d1dc9ce79c88

Chang, Lydia. "dear Lydia." *sincerely, lydia* (blog), September 12, 2018. https://sincerelydia.com/2018/09/12/dear-lydia/.

DeFazio, Jeanne, and John P. Lathrop. *Creative Ways to Build Christian Community*. Eugene, OR: Wipf and Stock, 2013.

DeFazio, Jeanne, and William David Spencer, editors. *Empowering English Language Learners: Successful Strategies of Christian Educators*. Eugene, OR: Wipf and Stock, 2018.

———, editors. *Redeeming the Screens: Living Stories of Media "Ministers" Bringing the Message of Jesus Christ to the Entertainment Industry*. Eugene, OR: Wipf and Stock, 2016.

Farnsworth, David Graham. "Interventions for Children with Mental Health Problems." Bright Hub Education. https://www.brighthubeducation.com/special-ed-inclusion-strategies/125590-interventions-for-students-with-mental-health-problems/.

Flowers, Teresa, and Jeanne DeFazio. *How to Have an Attitude of Gratitude on the Night Shift*. Eugene, OR: Resource, 2014.

Frooks, Dorothy. "Her Dream Needs Realism." *Murray Hill News*, 1986.

Healy, Patrick. "For John Glenn, a Rare Repeat Tour of the Canyon of Heroes." *New York TImes*, December 9, 2016. https://www.nytimes.com/2016/12/09/us/astronaut-john-glenn-death-nyc-parades-broadway.html.

Kleefeld, Sean. "Where Does 'Marvel Comics' Come From?" *Kleefeld on Comics* (blog), June 10, 2012. http://www.kleefeldoncomics.com/2012/06/where-does-marvel-comics-come-from.html.

The Learning Network. "Charles Lindbergh Flies Solo Across the Atlantic." *New York Times*, May 21, 2012. https://learning.blogs.nytimes.com/2012/05/21/may-21-1927-charles-lindbergh-flies-solo-across-the-atlantic/.

Madigan, Tim. "Van Cliburn: The Texan Who Conquered Russia." *Fort Worth Star-Telegram*, February 27, 2013. https://www.star-telegram.com/living/family/moms/article3834080.html.

Maeder, Jay. “The Day New York City Threw Charles Lindbergh a Ticker-Tape Parade for Soaring Nonstop to Paris in the Spirit of St. Louis.” *New York Daily News*, August 14, 2017. https://www.nydailynews.com/new-york/day-nyc-threw-charles-lindbergh-ticker-tape-parade-article-1.802575.

Mother Teresa. “Acceptance Speech.” Delivered December 10, 1979. https://www.nobelprize.org/prizes/peace/1979/teresa/acceptance-speech/.

Priestley, Chris. “Ignorance and Want: Why Charles Dickens's *A Christmas Carol* Is as Relevant Today As Ever.” *The Guardian*, December 23, 2015. https://www.theguardian.com/childrens-books-site/2015/dec/23/ignorance-and-want-why-charles-dickenss-a-christmas-carol-is-as-relevant-today-as-ever.

Procknow, Gene. “General Israel Putnam: Reputation Revisited.” Journal of the American Revolution, August 11, 2016. https://allthingsliberty.com/2016/08/general-israel-putnam-reputation-revisited/.

“A Short History of Japanese Manga.” *Widewalls*, editorial, September 24, 2016. https://www.widewalls.ch/japanese-manga-comics-history/.

Soler, Olga. *Apocalypse of Youth*. Bolton: Leap Over the Edge, 2017.

Stan Lee Biography.” Biography.com, A&E Television Networks. https://www.biography.com/people/stan-lee-21101093.

Vann, Madeline R. “Dealing with Depression and Loneliness.” Everyday Health, August 6, 2012. https://www.everydayhealth.com/hs/major-depression/depression-feeling-lonely/.

Walsh, Bryan. “Frankenstorm: Why Hurricane Sandy Will Be Historic, Time.” *Time*, October 29, 2012. http://science.time.com/2012/10/29/frankenstorm-why-hurricane-sandy-will-be-historic/.

Wang, Karen. “The Importance of the Arts in Special Education.” Friendship Circle, April 3, 2014. https://www.friendshipcircle.org/blog/2014/04/03/the-importance-of-the-arts-in-special-education/.

About the Authors

JULIA DAVIS has an EdM from the Harvard Graduate School of Education and an EdM from Bouve College of Health Sciences at Northwestern University. She has held teaching certificates in New York, Massachusetts, and the District of Columbia and has been certified as an assistant principal and as an assistant Special Education supervisor. Julia has taught in the public and private sector in community-based programs including METCO, summer STEP opportunities for underrepresented populations in science and technology, and Head Start. She has served as a member of the Parent's Advocacy Group for Massachusetts supporting FAPE and mainstreaming Special Education students. She has taught pre-K through grade 12, Adult Non-Readers, Limited English Language Learners, and GEDpreparation courses. Julia taught internationally as an undergraduate exchange student in a Special Education program based in Newnham on Severn, Gloucestershire, England, which operated under the auspices of Antioch College in Ohio. Julia and her husband, Dan, have three children and three grandchildren. They attend the International Family Church in North Reading, Massachusetts. Julia developed a monthly prayer breakfast program for the Everett, Massachusetts community.[1]

JEANNE DEFAZIO is a SAG/AFTRA actress of Spanish/Italian descent, who played supporting parts in theater, movies, and television series and disappeared into a life of service to the marginalized in the drama of real life. Jeanne became a teacher of Second Language Learner children in the barrios of San Diego. A woman of great faith, intelligence, and energy, she completed a Bachelor of Arts in history at the University of California, Davis, pursued seminary education at Gordon-Conwell Theological Seminary

1. DeFazio and Spencer, eds., *Empowering English Language Learners*, 150–51.

(MAR in theology), and completed a CalState TEACH English Language Learners program. In 2009 to present, Jeanne has returned as an Athanasian Teaching Scholar at Gordon Conwell's multicultural Boston Center for Urban Ministerial Education (CUME), which serves the often unnoticed but thriving ethnic churches. [2]

Email Jeanne at jcdefazio55@gmail.com.

Martha Reyes was born in Puerto Rico and has resided in California, ministering to Hispanics in the United States and internationally since 1978. She has traveled to more than twenty-two Latin American countries and many parts of Europe and the Middle East giving concerts and retreats on inner healing and participating as a guest speaker in national and international conventions on healing and restoration. From 1992 until 2000 she organized the acclaimed Hosanna Multifestival conventions, international events with representatives from thirty countries in music, theatre, and arts, held annually in Mexico, Florida, and Israel.[3]

Olga Soler is director/writer and performer for Estuary Ministries, a Christ-centered performing arts ministry dealing with biblical themes, inner healing, abuse, and addictive problems. The art forms used include drama, dance, storytelling, mime, comedy, graphic arts, writing, film, and song. Olga attended the High School of Performing Arts ("Fame"), the Lee Strasberg Theater Institute, and the Herbert Berghof Studios, in New York City. She has performed widely at conferences, churches, prisons, coffee houses, support groups, youth groups, and retreats and has even performed on the streets, at secular colleges, and in worship services across the United States and the United Kingdom. She holds degrees in education and communications with equivalent studies in theology and psychology. She studied for two years at Gordon Conwell Theological Seminary. She has designed and conducted the workshops "Dance Alive" and "Trauma Drama" at many Christian recovery conferences. She wrote the curriculum for and conducted discovery groups for addicts at the Boston Rescue Mission, using the arts to help them process aspects of their recovery. She also conducts workshops for Christian drama and dance in many churches of all denominations. Using Paulo Freire's "pedagogy of the oppressed," she wrote a script for the "Mosaics" group of parents helping their children

2. Flowers and DeFazio, *How to Have an Attitude of Gratitude on the Night Shift*, viii–ix.

3. DeFazio and Spencer, eds., Redeeming *the Screens*, 90–91.

who have been victims of sexual abuse through the court system and assisted them in filming the script for a documentary. She performed and coauthored scripts for four years with the "Team" Christian ministry in Massachusetts and conducted eight full-scale multimedia presentations out of the Rio Ondo Arts Place in Woburn, Massachusetts, including "Voice of the Martyrs," "Techno Easter," and "Clean Comedy Night." She has directed and choreographed entire productions at universities and colleges, including *A Man for All Seasons*, *Jane Eyre*, *Amal and the Night Visitors*, and (by permission of the author) Calvin Miller's *The Singer*. She wrote and illustrated the book *Epistle to the Magadalenes* and has conducted retreats for women using the book accompanied by dramatic presentation. She is the author of many other books and assorted screenplays. She is the proud mother of three wonderful children, Cielo, Reva, and Ransom. She lives in Massachusetts with her husband, Chris, and her Japanese Chin (dog), Kiji.[4]

Email Olga at fleursavag@yahoo.com,

William David Spencer is Distinguished Adjunct Professor of Theology and the Arts at Gordon-Conwell Theological Seminary's Boston campus/Center for Urban Ministerial Education (CUME). He has been teaching formally in a variety of educational institutions since 1968. He won the Nancy Higginson Dore Prize for excellence in education at Rutgers University, where he earned his bachelors in English education, certifying him as a secondary education English teacher, and he became serious about his faith in Jesus Christ at the Rutgers/Douglass InterVarsity Christian Fellowship. In college, he did his first street evangelism and with friends started an evangelistic band, The Spheres, performing across the eastern seaboard. After a blessed year studying at the former Philadelphia center of Gordon-Conwell, he earned a Master of Divinity degree with a New Testament concentration in the Greek and Hebrew track at Princeton Theological Seminary, while the band's ministry expanded, and he also did city ministry in Newark, New Jersey with Crosscounter Inc. and in West Philadelphia with Ethos and the Presbytery of Philadelphia, setting up block associations to bring racial reconciliation, and he helped set up and run two evangelistic coffeehouses. At the same time he co-led an evangelistic gospel band sponsored by the ministry of opera singer Jerome Hines.

After graduating, he became the Protestant chaplain at Rider College (now University), and was ordained as a Presbyterian minister. He also

4. DeFazio and Lathrop, *Creative Ways to Build Christian Community*, 86-87.

volunteered at a ministry his wife began in Trenton State Prison with Hispanic inmates. As he and his wife were completing their ThM degrees in Christian higher education, also at Princeton Theological Seminary, they were called back to Newark to teach basic Bible interpretation and supervise seminarians in urban ministry for New York Theological Seminary, Crosscounter Inc., and The Salvation Army Newark Central Corps. They created a college-level program, the Alpha-Omega Community Theological School (ACTS), for storefront pastors who were attending their courses, with four centers: two in Newark, one in Jersey City, and another in the Bedford Stuyvesant area of Brooklyn, working with The Salvation Army, The Church of God in Christ (COGIC), and The King's College. The program had one hundred students and fifteen professors. After that ministry closed, he accompanied his wife to Louisville, Kentucky so she could earn her doctorate. There he turned down an offer of another chaplaincy opportunity to fill in a gap in his education that troubled him in Newark: the ability to teach storefront pastors Greek but not theology because of the challenge of their reading level. So he chose instead to become a Laubach literacy teacher in a pioneering adult literacy program with the Jefferson County (Kentucky) Board of Education. After two years he became teaching coordinator for the county, where he established and supervised eight literacy and GED centers in the city of Louisville and surrounding towns. He also authored a pamphlet on how to begin a literacy center and coauthored a reading materials assessment booklet published by the Jefferson County Board of Education Adult Program. After his wife's graduation and invitation to teach at Gordon-Conwell Theological Seminary, he accompanied her to Massachusetts with their young son, Steve, and the next year was himself invited to offer courses for the school, while he helped re-establish the Evangelical Theological Society's Northeast section, serving two years as its chair and four years as its programmer, and co-planting Pilgrim Church, today a union church of the Conservative Congregational Christian Conference (4Cs) and the Cumberland Presbyterian Church (CPC), and he remains its founding Pastor of Encouragement. He also completed his Doctor of Theology (ThD) degree in theology and ancient literature at Boston University School of Theology. He is the author of more than two hundred articles, stories, poems, chapters in books, reviews, and editorials, and with his wife writes the blog *From the Timeless to the Timely: Applying Scriptural Truths Today.*[5]

5. DeFazio and Spencer, eds., *Empowering English Language Learners*, 156–57.

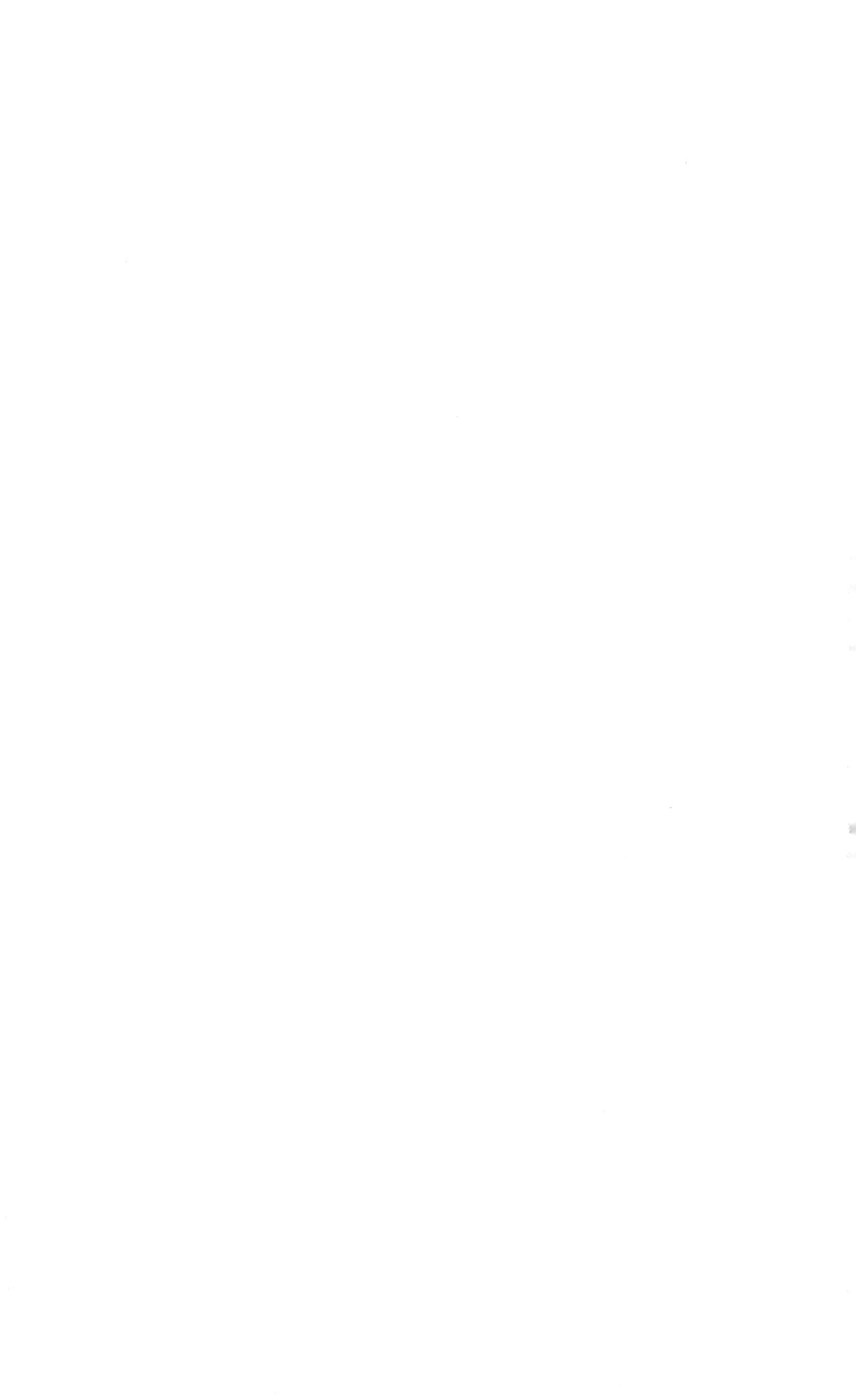

www.ingramcontent.com/pod-product-compliance
Lightning Source LLC
LaVergne TN
LVHW050543100826
845148LV00002B/661

* 9 7 8 1 5 3 2 6 8 4 2 8 9 *